A/75/27

General Assembly
Official Records
Seventy-fifth Session
Supplement No. 27

Report of the Conference on Disarmament

2020 session

United Nations • New York, 2020

Note

Symbols of United Nations documents are composed of letters combined with figures. Mention of such a symbol indicates a reference to a United Nations document.

Print ISSN 0257-0645
Online ISSN 1563-9029

Contents

I. Introduction

1.   The Conference on Disarmament submits to the seventy-fifth session of the General Assembly of the United Nations its annual report on its 2020 session, together with the pertinent documents and records.

II. Organization of the work of the Conference

A. 2020 session of the Conference

2.   The Conference was in session from 20 January to 27 March, 25 May to 10 July and 3 August to 18 September 2020. During this period, the Conference held 25 formal plenary meetings, at which member States as well as non-member States invited to participate in the discussions outlined their views and recommendations on the various issues before the Conference.

3.   The Conference also held 4 informal plenary meetings.

4.   The Presidency was assumed in accordance with rule 9 of the rules of procedure, as specified in the Appendix I to this report. The Conference noted that without creating a precedent for its future sessions the Presidents of 2020 invited the last President of the 2019 session and the first President of the 2021 session to attend their regular informal meetings for the sake of the continuity of the Conference's work.

5.   The Conference's work in 2020 was severely impacted by the COVID-19 pandemic, which resulted in a reduction in the number of plenary meetings and the alteration of their format. Whereas the first two Presidents of the Conference, Mr. Rachid Belbaki, Ambassador of Algeria, and Mr. Carlos Mario Foradori, Ambassador of Argentina, were able to hold regular plenary meetings, between 10 March and 29 June the Presidents of the Conference, Ms. Sally Mansfield, Ambassador of Australia, and Mr. Robert Müller, Ambassador of Austria, were not in the position to convene any plenary meetings due to the restrictions imposed in response to the pandemic. Subsequently, the UN secretariat was able to provide teleconference systems to allow the convening of plenary meetings in a 'hybrid' format with delegates participating both in person and remotely. Such meetings were convened on 30 June by the President of the Conference Mr. Robert Müller, Ambassador of Austria, on 13 August by the President of the Conference Mr. Shameem Ahsan, Ambassador of Bangladesh, and on 27 August, 8 September and 16 September by the President of the Conference Mr. Yury Ambrazevich, Ambassador of Belarus. The Conference noted that use of hybrid and virtual formats did not create a precedent for future Conference meetings, yet it proved to be a tool, which allowed the Conference to continue its work in the pandemic situation. The Conference noted with appreciation the efforts of the UN secretariat in putting in place the teleconference systems and encouraged the UN secretariat, in coordination with the Secretariat of the Conference, to continue their work on developing contingency plans to allow the Conference to maintain its work in extraordinary situations, whilst providing greater financial transparency to the Member States.

6.   At the 1525th plenary meeting on 28 January 2020, Ms. Tatiana Valovaya, Secretary-General of the Conference on Disarmament and Personal Representative of the Secretary-General of the United Nations, delivered a message on behalf of Secretary-General António Guterres (CD/PV.1525).

7.   In a letter dated 20 January 2020, the first President of the Conference, Mr. Rachid Belbaki, Ambassador of Algeria, and the Secretary-General of the Conference on Disarmament and Personal Representative of the Secretary-General of the United Nations, Ms. Tatiana Valovaya jointly invited member States to address the Conference on Disarmament at the ministerial level during the 2020 session. The following dignitaries addressed the Conference on Disarmament: Mr. Sabri Boukadoum, Minister for Foreign Affairs of Algeria (CD/PV.1523), Mr. Philippe Goffin, Minister for Foreign Affairs and Minister of Defense of Belgium (CD/PV.1532); Mr. Edgars Rinkēvičs, Minister of Foreign Affairs of Latvia (CD/PV.1532); Ms. Kang Kyung-wha, Minister of Foreign Affairs of the Republic of Korea (CD/PV.1532); Mr. Jean-Yves Le Drian, Ministre de l'Europe et des Affaires étrangères of France (CD/PV.1532); Mr. Jacek Czaputowicz, Minister of Foreign Affairs of the Republic of Poland (CD/PV.1532); Ann Linde, Minister of Foreign Affairs of Sweden (CD/PV.1532); Mr. Stef Blok, Minister of Foreign Affairs of the Kingdom of the Netherlands (CD/PV.1532); Mr. Faisal Al-Saud, Minister of Foreign Affairs of Saudi Arabia (CD/PV.1532); Ms. Arancha González Laya, Minister for Foreign Affairs, E.U. and Cooperation of Spain (CD/PV.1532); Mr. Mukhtar Tileuberdi, Minister of Foreign Affairs of the Republic of Kazakhstan (CD/PV.1532); Mr. Mohamed Ali Al-Hakim, Minister of Foreign Affairs of the Republic of Iraq (CD/PV.1532); Mr. Pekka Haavisto, Minister of Foreign Affairs of Finland (CD/PV.1533); Mr. Ehab Fawzy, Assistant Minister for Multilateral and International Security Affairs of the Arab Republic of Egypt (CD/PV.1533); Mr. Bruno Rodriguez Parrilla, Minister of Foreign Affairs of Cuba (CD/PV.1533); Mr. Fabio Marzano, Vice-Minister for Sovereignty and Citizenship of Brazil (CD/PV.1533); Mr. Simon Coveney, Tánaiste and Minister for Foreign Affairs and Trade of Ireland (CD/PV.1533); Ms. Lolwah Rashid Al Khater, Assistant Foreign Minister and spokesperson for the Ministry of Foreign Affairs of Qatar (CD/PV.1533); Ambassador (Dr.) Pankaj Sharma, Permanent Representative of India to the Conference on Disarmament (CD/PV.1533); Mr. Yury Ambrazevich, Ambassador and Permanent Representative of Belarus to the United Nations and Other International Organizations in Geneva (CD/PV.1533); Mr. Gordan Grlić Radman, Minister of Foreign and European Affairs of the Republic of Croatia (CD/PV.1534); Mr. Sergey Lavrov, Minister of Foreign Affairs of the Russian Federation (CD/PV.1534); Lord Ahmad of Wimbledon, Minister of State for Foreign and Commonwealth Affairs of the United Kingdom (CD/PV.1534); Mr. Nikolaos-Georgios Dendias, Minister of Foreign Affairs of the Hellenic Republic (CD/PV.1534); Ms. Asako Omi, Parliamentary Vice-Minister for Foreign Affairs of Japan (CD/PV.1534); Mr. Cornel Feruta, Deputy Minister of Foreign Affairs of Romania (CD/PV.1534); Mr. Erki Kodar, Deputy Minister of Foreign Affairs of Estonia (CD/PV.1534); Mr. Mohsen Baharvand, Deputy Foreign Minister for International and Legal Affairs of the Islamic Republic of Iran (CD/PV.1534); Mr. Ahmad Faisal bin Muhamad, Ambassador and Permanent Representative of Malaysia to the United Nations Office and other international organizations in Geneva (CD/PV.1534); Mr. Andreano Erwin, Ambassador and Deputy Permanent Representative of the Republic of Indonesia to the United Nations, the World Trade Organization and other international organizations in Geneva (CD/PV.1534); Mr. Matej Marn, Deputy Minister of Foreign Affairs of the Republic of Slovenia (CD/PV.1535); Mr. Alvin Botes, Deputy Minister of International Relations and Cooperation of the Republic of South Africa (CD/PV.1535); Mr. Alexander Yánez Deleuze, Vice-Minister for Multilateral Affairs of the Ministry of People's Power for Foreign Affairs of the Bolivarian Republic of Venezuela (CD/PV.1535); Mr. Pham Quang Hieu, Assistant to the Foreign Minister of Viet Nam (CD/PV.1538).

8.   In their addresses, these dignitaries variously voiced support for the Conference and the principles of multilateralism, as well as the critical importance of multilateral

diplomacy and multilateral institutions in the context of the United Nations, expressed concern about the Conference's current situation, called upon the Conference to do its part to advance the international agenda by overcoming its ongoing deadlock, and set out their national priorities for the work of the Conference.

9.   The substantive secretariat of the Conference on Disarmament was composed as follows: Ms. Tatiana Valovaya, Secretary-General of the Conference on Disarmament and Personal Representative of the Secretary-General of the United Nations; Ms. Anja Kaspersen, Deputy Secretary-General of the Conference on Disarmament and Director of the Geneva Branch, United Nations Office for Disarmament Affairs; Ms. Radha Day, Senior Political Affairs Officer and Secretary of the Conference on Disarmament; Ms. Silvia Mercogliano, Political Affairs Officer; Ms. Erika Kawahara, Associate Political Affairs Officer and Mr. Yao Yue, Associate Political Affairs Officer.

B.   Participants in the work of the Conference

10.   The representatives of the following 65 member States participated in the work of the Conference: Algeria, Argentina, Australia, Austria, Bangladesh, Belarus, Belgium, Brazil, Bulgaria, Cameroon, Canada, Chile, China, Colombia, Cuba, Democratic People's Republic of Korea, Democratic Republic of the Congo, Ecuador, Egypt, Ethiopia, Finland, France, Germany, Hungary, India, Indonesia, Iran (Islamic Republic of), Iraq, Ireland, Israel, Italy, Japan, Kazakhstan, Kenya, Malaysia, Mexico, Mongolia, Morocco, Myanmar, Netherlands, New Zealand, Nigeria, Norway, Pakistan, Peru, Poland, Republic of Korea, Romania, Russian Federation, Senegal, Slovakia, South Africa, Spain, Sri Lanka, Sweden, Switzerland, Syrian Arab Republic, Tunisia, Turkey, Ukraine, United Kingdom of Great Britain and Northern Ireland, United States of America, Venezuela (Bolivarian Republic of), Viet Nam and Zimbabwe.

C.   Attendance and participation of States not members of the Conference

11.   In accordance with the rules of procedure and the decision taken at its 1990 session on its improved and effective functioning (CD/1036), the Conference received and considered 42 requests for participation in its work. Discussion on the subject is reflected in the CD/PV.1523, the relevant part of which is contained in Appendix II.

12.   The Conference invited the following non-member States to participate in its work: Afghanistan, Albania, Angola, Armenia, Azerbaijan, Bosnia and Herzegovina, Cambodia, Chad, Costa Rica, Côte d'Ivoire, Croatia, Czech Republic, Dominican Republic, Estonia, Georgia, Ghana, Greece, Guatemala, Holy See, Honduras, Jordan, Kuwait, Latvia, Lebanon, Lithuania, Luxemburg, Malta, Montenegro, North Macedonia, Panama, Philippines, Portugal, Qatar, Republic of Moldova, Saudi Arabia, Serbia, Singapore, Slovenia, Sudan, Thailand, Trinidad and Tobago.

D.   Agenda and programme of work for the 2020 session

13.   At its 1523rd plenary meeting on 21 January 2020, a draft agenda was presented by the President of the Conference, Mr. Rachid Belbaki, Ambassador of Algeria, and reviewed in accordance with rule 29 of the rules of procedure. The Conference on Disarmament adopted the following agenda (CD/2183) for the 2020 session (CD/PV.1523):

"Taking into account, inter alia, the relevant provisions of the Final Document of the First Special Session of the General Assembly devoted to disarmament, and deciding to resume its consultations on the review of its agenda, and without prejudice to their outcome, the Conference adopts the following agenda for its 2020 session:

1. Cessation of the nuclear arms race and nuclear disarmament.

2. Prevention of nuclear war, including all related matters.

3. Prevention of an arms race in outer space.

4. Effective international arrangements to assure non-nuclear-weapon States against the use or threat of use of nuclear weapons.

5. New types of weapons of mass destruction and new systems of such weapons; radiological weapons.

6. Comprehensive programme of disarmament.

7. Transparency in armaments.

8. Consideration and adoption of the annual report and any other report, as appropriate, to the General Assembly of the United Nations."

14. Subsequently, the President made the following statement: "In connection with the adoption of the agenda, I, as the President of the Conference, should like to state that it is my understanding that if there is a consensus in the Conference to deal with any issues, they could be dealt with within this agenda. The Conference will also take into consideration rules 27 and 30 of the rules of procedure of the Conference."

15. Pursuant to paragraph 45 of the 2019 report of the Conference (CD/2179), the last President of the 2019 session (Zimbabwe) and the first President of the 2020 session (Algeria), conducted informal consultations during the intersessional period with a view to commencing early substantive work during the 2020 session of the Conference.

16. Throughout the 2020 session, Presidents of the Conference conducted intensive consultations with a view to reaching consensus on a programme of work on the basis of the relevant proposals, namely presented by the President of the Conference, Mr. Rachid Belbaki, Ambassador of Algeria, and by the President of the Conference, Mr. Carlos Mario Foradori, Ambassador of Argentina. Delegations expressed their views on the issue of a programme of work, taking account of relevant proposals and suggestions, which are duly reflected in the plenary records. However, despite these efforts, the Conference did not succeed in reaching consensus on a programme of work in 2020.

17. The following documents were submitted to the Conference:

(a) CD/2187;

(b) CD/2187/Add.1;

(c) CD/2187/Add.2;

(d) CD/2187/Add.3;

(e) CD/2189.

E. Expansion of the membership of the Conference

18   The question of the expansion of the membership of the Conference was addressed by delegations in plenary meetings. Their views on the issue are duly reflected in the plenary records.

19.   Since 1982, requests for membership have been received from the following 27 non-members, in chronological order: Greece, Croatia, Kuwait, Portugal, Slovenia, Czech Republic, Costa Rica, Denmark, North Macedonia, Cyprus, Lithuania, Ghana, Luxembourg, Uruguay, Philippines, Azerbaijan, Libya, Armenia, Thailand, Georgia, Jordan, Estonia, Latvia, Malta, Serbia, Republic of Moldova and Qatar.

F. Review of the agenda of the Conference

20.   The review of the agenda of the Conference was addressed by delegations in plenary meetings. Their views on the issue are duly reflected in the plenary records.

G. Improved and effective functioning of the Conference

21.   The improved and effective functioning of the Conference was addressed by delegations in plenary meetings. Their views on the issue are duly reflected in the plenary records.

H. Conference and the non-governmental organizations

22.   During the general debate, delegations reaffirmed or further elaborated their respective positions on the Conference's interaction with civil society. Their views are duly reflected in the plenary records of the Conference.

23.   The virtual informal event "Conference on Disarmament meets civil society. Lessons of the Pandemic: Rethinking the nexus between disarmament and security" was co-convened by the President of the Conference, Mr. Robert Müller, Ambassador of Austria, and the Secretary-General of the Conference on Disarmament Ms. Tatiana Valovaya on 3 July 2020.

III. Substantive work of the Conference during its 2020 session

24.   During the general debate of the Conference, delegations affirmed or further elaborated their respective positions on the agenda items. These positions are duly recorded in the plenary records of the session.

25.   The list of documents issued by the Conference are included as Appendix III to this report. Verbatim records of the formal plenary meetings of the Conference and related information as to country and subject is digitally available online.

26.   The Conference had before it a letter dated 2 January 2020 from the Secretary-General of the United Nations transmitting the resolutions and decisions on disarmament and international security matters adopted by the General Assembly at its seventy-fourth session in 2019, including those making specific reference to the Conference on Disarmament (CD/2184). The latter are listed below:

74/31   Conclusion of effective international arrangements to assure non-nuclear-weapon States against the use or threat of use of nuclear weapons (Tenth, twelfth, thirteenth, and sixteenth preambular paragraphs; operative paragraphs 2, 4, and 5)

74/32   Prevention of an arms race in outer space (Sixth, eleventh, seventeenth, eighteenth, nineteenth and twenty-first preambular paragraphs; operative paragraphs 5, 6, and 8)

74/33   No first placement of weapons in outer space (Ninth preambular paragraph; operative paragraphs 2 and 3)

74/34   Further practical measures for the prevention of an arms race in outer space (Eighth and tenth preambular paragraphs, operative paragraphs 4 and 5)

74/35   Role of science and technology in the context of international security and disarmament (Seventh preambular paragraph)

74/37   Regional disarmament (Operative paragraph 1)

74/38   Conventional arms control at the regional and subregional levels (Operative paragraph 2)

74/45   Nuclear disarmament (Sixteenth, eighteenth, nineteenth, twentieth, and twenty-first preambular paragraphs; operative paragraphs 16, 17, and 20)

74/46   Towards a nuclear-weapon-free world: accelerating the implementation of nuclear disarmament commitments (Twenty-third preambular paragraph; operative paragraph 17)

74/47   Ethical imperatives for a nuclear-weapon free world (Ninth preambular paragraph)

74/50   Nuclear disarmament verification (First preambular paragraph, operative paragraphs 3 and 9)

74/53   Transparency in armaments (Operative paragraphs 6 and 9)

74/54   Follow-up to the 2013 high-level meeting of the General Assembly on nuclear disarmament (Fifteenth preambular paragraph; operative paragraphs 4, 6, and 13)

74/58   Prohibition of the dumping of radioactive wastes (Ninth preambular paragraph; operative paragraphs 1, 2, 5 and 6)

74/59   Follow-up to the advisory opinion of the International Court of Justice on the legality of the threat or use of nuclear weapons (Thirteenth and fourteenth preambular paragraphs)

74/63   Joint Courses of Action and Future-oriented Dialogue towards a world without nuclear weapons (Eighth preambular paragraph, operative paragraph 3(c), 3(e), and 4(a))

74/67   Transparency and confidence-building measures in outer space activities (Sixth and seventh preambular paragraphs; operative paragraph 3)

74/68   Convention on the Prohibition of the Use of Nuclear Weapons (Ninth preambular paragraph; operative paragraphs 1 and 2)

74/69   United Nations Regional Centre for Peace and Disarmament in Asia and the Pacific (Third preambular paragraph)

74/74   Report of the Conference on Disarmament (First, second, fourth, fifth, sixth, seventh, and tenth preambular paragraphs, operative paragraphs 1, 2, 3, 4, 5, 6, 7, 8, and 9)

27.   The following documents were submitted to the Conference:

(a)   CD/2191;

(b)   CD/2197;

(c)   CD/2198.

A. Cessation of the nuclear arms race and nuclear disarmament

28.   During the general debate of the Conference, delegations reaffirmed or further elaborated their respective positions on this agenda item. These positions are duly recorded in the plenary records of the session.

29.   The following documents were submitted to the Conference under this agenda item:

(a)   CD/2180;

(b)   CD/2182;

(c)   CD/2185;

(d)   CD/2186;

(e)   CD/2188;

(f)   CD/2192;

(g)   CD/2195.

B. Prevention of nuclear war, including all related matters

30.   During the general debate of the Conference, delegations reaffirmed or further elaborated their respective positions on this agenda item. These positions are duly recorded in the plenary records of the session.

31.   The following documents were submitted to the Conference under this agenda item:

(a)   CD/2180;

(b)   CD/2182;

(c)   CD/2185;

(d)   CD/2186;

(e)   CD/2188;

(f)   CD/2192;

(g)   CD/2195.

C. Prevention of an arms race in outer space

32.   During the general debate of the Conference, delegations reaffirmed or further elaborated their respective positions on this agenda item. These positions are duly recorded in the plenary records of the session.

33.   The following documents were submitted to the Conference under this agenda item:

(a)   CD/2181;

(b)   CD/2193.

D. Effective international arrangements to assure non-nuclear-weapon States against the use or threat of use of nuclear weapons

34.   During the general debate of the Conference, delegations reaffirmed or further elaborated their respective positions on this agenda item. These positions are duly recorded in the plenary records of the session.

35.   The following document was submitted to the Conference under this agenda item:

CD/2194.

E. New types of weapons of mass destruction and new systems of such weapons; radiological weapons

36.   During the general debate of the Conference, delegations reaffirmed or further elaborated their respective positions on this agenda item. These positions are duly recorded in the plenary records of the session.

37.   Thematic plenary discussion on the agenda items 5, 6, 7 was convened by the President of the Conference, Mr. Yury Ambrazevich, Ambassador of Belarus.

38.   The following document was submitted to the Conference under this agenda item:

CD/2199.

F. Comprehensive programme of disarmament

39.   During the general debate of the Conference, delegations reaffirmed or further elaborated their respective positions on this agenda item. These positions are duly recorded in the plenary records of the session.

40.   Thematic plenary discussion on the agenda items 5, 6, 7 was convened by the President of the Conference, Mr. Yury Ambrazevich, Ambassador of Belarus.

G. Transparency in armaments

41.   During the general debate of the Conference, delegations reaffirmed or further elaborated their respective positions on this agenda item. These positions are duly recorded in the plenary records of the session.

42. Thematic plenary discussion on the agenda items 5, 6, 7 was convened by the President of the Conference, Mr. Yury Ambrazevich, Ambassador of Belarus.

H. Consideration of other areas dealing with the cessation of the arms race and disarmament and other relevant measures

43. The following documents were submitted to the Conference:

    (a)   CD/2190;

    (b)   CD/2196.

I. Consideration and adoption of the annual report of the Conference and any other report as appropriate to the General Assembly of the United Nations

44. Being aware of the need for progress in fulfilling the mandate of the Conference, and building on the focused efforts in the Conference on Disarmament to establish a programme of work for the 2020 session and with a view to early commencement of substantive work during its 2021 session, the Conference requested the current President and the incoming President to conduct consultations during the intersessional period and, if possible, make recommendations taking into account all relevant proposals, past, present and future, including those submitted as documents of the Conference on Disarmament, views presented and discussions held, and to endeavour to keep the membership of the Conference informed, as appropriate, of their consultations.

45. The Conference decided that the dates for its 2021 session would be:

First part:	18 January – 26 March
Second part:	10 May – 25 June
Third part:	26 July – 10 September.

46. The annual report to the seventy-fifth session of the General Assembly of the United Nations, as adopted by the Conference on 18 September 2020, is transmitted by the President on behalf of the Conference on Disarmament.

(*Signed*) Ambassador Yury **Ambrazevich**
Belarus
President of the Conference

Appendix I

Names of the CD members that served as the Presidents of the 2020 session

Algeria
Argentina
Australia
Austria
Bangladesh
Belarus

Appendix II

Extracted from CD/PV.1523

The President (spoke in French): We will now decide on the request from Cyprus. May I take it that the Conference decides to grant this request to take part in our deliberations in accordance with our rules of procedure? I give the floor to the representative of Turkey.

Mr. Ağacıkoğlu (Turkey): Thank you, Mr. President. At the outset I would like to congratulate you on your assumption of the first presidency of the Conference on Disarmament in 2020. I assure you of Turkey's full support and cooperation in your efforts to advance the work of the Conference.

Mr. President, as it might be recalled, although Turkey has had concerns with this particular request, we have never objected to a blanket list or chosen to block a country on the list from participating as an observer of Conference activities. Instead, we have registered our position with a letter afterwards. This course of action was due to the utmost importance that Turkey has attached to not spoiling or politicizing the positive atmosphere of the Conference. Nevertheless, we all witnessed together last year that, in that respect, the Rubicon has already been crossed. Therefore, Turkey also decided to stop exercising restraint on this particular matter. Herewith, then, I would like to declare that Turkey will not support this particular request this year.

The President (spoke in French): In the light of the objection raised, we do not have a consensus to allow Cyprus to participate as an observer in the 2020 session of the Conference. The request is therefore rejected.

Appendix III

List and texts of documents issued by the Conference on Disarmament

Document No.	Title
CD/2180	Note verbale dated 13 September 2019 from the Permanent Mission of the Republic of Kazakhstan addressed to the Secretariat of the Conference on Disarmament and conveying the Chair's summary of the Seminar on Fostering Cooperation and Enhancing Consultation Mechanisms Among the Existing Nuclear-Weapon-Free-Zones, which was held on August 28–29, 2019 in Nur-Sultan, Kazakhstan.
CD/2181	Letter dated 23 October 2019 from the Permanent Representative of the Russian Federation addressed to the Secretary-General of the of the Conference on Disarmament, Ms. Tatiana Valovaya, transmitting the text of the Joint Statement of the CIS States Parties on Supporting Practical Steps to Prevent an Arms Race in Outer Space adopted by the CIS States Parties' Ministers of Foreign Affairs on October 10, 2019
CD/2182	Note verbale dated 13 December 2019 from the Special Representation of Brazil to the Conference on Disarmament, in its capacity of President of the Council of the Agency for the Prohibition of Nuclear Weapons in Latin America and the Caribbean (OPANAL), addressed to the Secretariat of the Conference on Disarmament transmitting the OPANAL Declaration on the International Day for the Complete Elimination of Nuclear Weapons and requesting issuance of this document as an official document of the Conference on Disarmament
CD/2183	Agenda for the 2020 session. (Adopted at the 1523rd plenary meeting on 21 January 2020)
CD/2184	Letter dated 2 January 2020 from the Secretary-General of the United Nations addressed to the President of the Conference on Disarmament transmitting the resolutions and decisions on disarmament and international security matters adopted by the General Assembly at its seventy-fourth session
CD/2185	Note Verbale dated 14 February 2020 from the Permanent Mission of Mexico, transmitting a copy of the "Communiqué of the Member States of the Agency for the Prohibition of Nuclear Weapons in Latin America and the Caribbean (OPANAL) on the 53rd Anniversary of the Treaty of Tlatelolco" (Inf. 02/2020 Rev.7), dated 12 February 2020
CD/2186	Note Verbale dated 10 March 2020 from the Permanent Mission of Belarus, transmitting Statement by the Ministry of Foreign Affairs of the Republic of Belarus on the occasion of the 50th anniversary of the entry into force of the Treaty on the Non-Proliferation of Nuclear Weapons

Document No.	Title
CD/2187	Note Verbale dated 25 March 2020 from the Permanent Mission of Australia addressed to the Secretariat of the Conference on Disarmament and requesting to register the three packages proposed by the six Presidents of the 2020 session of the Conference on Disarmament (P6) and circulated on 13 and 24 February 2020 and on 2 March 2020 as official documents of the Conference on Disarmament
CD/2187/Add.1	Package circulated on 13 February 2020 comprising a draft Presidential Statement on the improved and effective functioning of the Conference; the revised CD/WP.626/Rev.1 on the draft proposal for a programme of work of the Conference on Disarmament for 2020; and the CD/WP.627 on a draft decision for the implementation of the programme of work
CD/2187/Add.2	Revised package circulated on 24 February 2020 comprising a draft Presidential Statement on the improved and effective functioning of the Conference; the revised CD/WP.626/Rev.2 on the draft proposal for a programme of work of the Conference on Disarmament for 2020; and the CD/WP.627/Rev.1 on a draft decision for the implementation of the programme of work
CD/2187/Add.3	Revised package circulated on 2 March 2020 comprising a draft Presidential Statement on the improved and effective functioning of the Conference; the revised CD/WP.626/Rev.3 on the draft proposal on the work of the Conference on Disarmament for 2020; and the CD/WP.627/Rev.2 on a draft decision for the implementation of the work of the Conference on Disarmament for 2020
CD/2188	Note Verbale dated 30 April 2020 from the Permanent Mission of the Russian Federation, transmitting Statement by the Foreign Ministry of the Russian Federation concerning the 10th anniversary of the signing of the Treaty on Measures for the Further Reduction and Limitation of Strategic Offensive Arms (New START)
CD/2189	Note Verbale dated 27 April 2020 from the Permanent Mission of the Islamic Republic of Iran transmitting the amendments proposed by the Islamic Republic of Iran to the Proposed Draft Programme of Work of the Conference on Disarmament for 2020 during the Plenary meetings of the First Part of the 2020 Session of the Conference on Disarmament
CD/2190	Note Verbale dated 13 August 2020 from the Permanent Mission of Ukraine transmitting the Commentary of the Ministry of Foreign Affairs of Ukraine of August 12, 2020 in connection with the illegal military exercises of the Black Sea fleet of the Russian Federation in the territories of the temporarily occupied Autonomous Republic of Crimea and the city of Sevastopol
CD/2191	General Statement. Submitted by the Group of 21 (G-21)
CD/2192	Statement on Nuclear Disarmament. Submitted by the Group of 21 (G-21)

Document No.	Title
CD/2193 and Corr.1	Statement on the Prevention of an Arms Race in Outer Space (PAROS). Submitted by the Group of 21 (G-21)
CD/2194	Statement on negative Security Assurances. Submitted by the Group of 21 (G-21)
CD/2195	Statement on Follow-up to the 2013 High Level Meeting of the General Assembly of Nuclear Disarmament. Submitted by the Group of 21 (G-21)
CD/2196	Letter dated 18 August 2020 from the Permanent Representative of the Russian Federation addressed to the Secretary-General of the Conference on Disarmament, transmitting the text of the Statement by the President of the Russian Federation H.E. Vladimir V. Putin on Russia's proposal to convene meetings of Heads of State of the United Nations Security Council permanent members with participation of Heads of State of Germany and Iran presented by the Minister of Foreign Affairs of the Russian Federation H.E. Sergey Lavrov on August 14, 2020.
CD/2197	Summary of consultations during Australia's Presidency. Submitted by the Permanent Mission of Australia
CD/2198	Australian proposal to make the Conference on Disarmament Rules of Procedure gender neutral
CD/2199	Note Verbale dated 8 September from the Permanent Mission of the Republic of Belarus addressed to the Secretariat of the Conference on Disarmament and transmitting the Draft Resolution of the United Nations General Assembly "Prohibition of the development and manufacture of new types of weapons of mass destruction and new systems of such weapons: report of the Conference on Disarmament"
CD/2200	Note Verbale dated 16 September from the Permanent Mission of the Russian Federation addressed to the Secretariat of the Conference on Disarmament and transmitting the Statement of the Russian Federation concerning a commentary by the MFA of Ukraine dated 12 August 2020
CD/2201	Note Verbale dated 16 September from the Permanent Mission of Germany addressed to the Secretariat of the Conference on Disarmament and transmitting the Statement delivered by the Permanent Representative of Germany, Ambassador Peter Beerwerth, at the 1546th Plenary meeting of the Conference on Disarmament on 16 September 2020
CD/2202	Note Verbale dated 17 September from the Permanent Mission of Sweden addressed to the Secretariat of the Conference on Disarmament and transmitting the Statement delivered by Sweden at the 1546th Plenary meeting of the Conference on Disarmament on 16 September 2020

Document No.	Title
CD/2203	Note Verbale dated 17 September from the Permanent Mission of the United States addressed to the Secretariat of the Conference on Disarmament and transmitting the Statement delivered by the Permanent Representative of the United States, Ambassador Robert A. Wood, at the 1546th Plenary meeting of the Conference on Disarmament on 16 September 2020
CD/2204	Note Verbale dated 18 September from the Permanent Mission of the Russian Federation addressed to the Secretary-General of the of the Conference on Disarmament and transmitting the Commentary of the Informal and Press Department of the Ministry of Foreign Affairs of the Russian Federation concerning the situation with Mr. Alexei Navalny.
CD/2205	Note Verbale dated 16 September from the Permanent Mission of the Islamic Republic of Iran addressed to the Secretariat of the Conference on Disarmament and transmitting Statements delivered by the delegation of the Islamic Republic of Iran at the 1543rd and 1546th Plenary meetings of the Conference of Disarmament on 13 of August and 16 September 2020
CD/2206	Note Verbale dated 18 September 2020 from the Permanent Mission of Israel addressed to the Secretariat of the Conference on Disarmament and transmitting the Statement delivered by the delegation of Israel at the 1543rd Plenary meeting of the Conference on Disarmament on 13 August 2020
CD/2207	Report of the Conference on Disarmament to the General Assembly of the United Nations

20-12776 (E)   011020